ALSO AVAILABLE IN
THE WISDOM OF SERIES

ANCIENT GREECE

Compiled by Jacques Lacarrière
Photographs by Jacques Lacarrière

ANCIENT ROME

Compiled by Benoît Desombres

ISLAM

Compiled by Nacer Khémir

JESUS

Compiled by Jean-Yves Leloup

JUDAISM

Compiled by Victor Malka
Illustrations by Marc Chagall

TAO

Compiled by Marc de Smedt

ZEN

Compiled by Marc de Smedt
Calligraphy by Master Taisen Deshimaru

THE WISDOM OF
BUDDHA

Compiled by Marc de Smedt
Photography by Jean-Louis Nou

Abbeville Press Publishers
New York London Paris

Cover illustration and vignettes by Danielle Siegelbaum

For the English-language edition
RESEARCH, TRANSLATION FROM THE FRENCH, AND BIBLIOGRAPHY:
John O'Toole
EDITOR: Jacqueline Decter
TYPOGRAPHIC DESIGN: Virginia Pope
PRODUCTION EDITOR: Owen Dugan

For the original edition
SERIES EDITORS: Marc de Smedt and Michel Piquemal

First edition
10 9 8 7 6 5 4 3 2 1

Library of Congress Cataloging-in-Publication Data

Paroles du Bouddha. English.
The wisdom of the Buddha/compiled by Marc de Smedt; pho-
tographs by Jean-Louis Nou.
p. cm.
Includes bibliographical references.
ISBN 0-7892-0238-7
1. Gautama Buddha—Teachings. I. Smedt, Marc de, 1946–   . II.
Nou, Jean Louis. III. Title.
BQ915.P3613 1996
294.3'63—dc20   96–21499

Siddhartha Gautama, later called the Buddha, the Enlightened One, was born some twenty-five hundred years ago in the northern Indian town of Lumbini, not far from the present-day border with Nepal. His father is said to have been a king. Archeological digs in the area have enabled us to determine that he was indeed a lord, a kind of head of a clan, the Sakyas. He was born into a powerful family, the Gautamas, whose means of existence were far superior to those of the common people. Legend also has it that his father, concerned by a prediction a hermit had made at the boy's birth to the effect that he would become either a great king or a great sage, apparently did all in his power to make the first part of the prophesy come true. Young Prince Siddhartha was given an advanced intellectual and military education, and his father did everything he could to spare his son all care. Women dancers, hunts, tutors, and servants filled the young man's waking hours. A marriage was also arranged with the daughter of a neighboring clan, the pretty Yasodhara, who bore him a son. Yet all of this still did not make for his happiness. He was tormented and depressed by the existence of disease, dire poverty, old age, and death, which "took away all pride in the life [he] was leading," a life whose futility he could feel. Thus one night he abandoned palace and family, and fled far from the easy life to search for truth and attempt to understand the meaning of existence. He was thirty years old. He cut his long hair, cast off his fine clothes for a simple tunic, and left to follow the teachings dispensed by the sages of his day. For years he practiced the techniques of yoga, fasted, and heeded various philosophies, yet without quelling his desire to understand. He decided to shut himself up in a cave and meditate until he discovered the underlying meaning of the world. He remained there until he became a kind of fantastic, unreal skeleton living on one grain of rice a day—still to no avail. With a start he left his cave, not wanting to die there like a dog in a hole, and dragged himself to a tree, where he leaned his back against the roots to pass away in broad daylight at least.

There he heard a music teacher sit down with his students in a nearby grove. The teacher said, "To make pleasant music a lute must be well tuned; if the strings are too slack, the sound is lifeless; if the strings are too taut, the sound is jarring. We must find the right accord." These words sparked true enlightenment in Gautama, for he realized that they applied to his own situation. As a prince, he had led a life that was too slack and decadent, while as a vagabond, he was leading a useless life that was bringing him to the brink of physical decay—again for nothing. He now understood that truth lies in the balance of forces, and thus discovered the first principle of what would become Buddhism: the way of the happy medium. Our body and being must be harmoniously in tune if we wish to function properly and be of use to others. A new life began for Gautama; while regaining his strength he continued to meditate for a long time before deciding to teach willing students what he called the Noble Path, a set of eight precepts that can still be helpful to us today: right understanding, right thought, right speech, right action, right livelihood, right effort, right mindfulness, and right concentration. He died at the age of eighty, giving birth to a new philosophy, one that would never lead to war.

Marc de Smedt

Jean-Louis Nou's photographs have been arranged chronologically to retrace the life of the Buddha.

The True Conqueror

Between him who in battle has conquered

thousands upon thousands of men,

and him who has conquered himself,

it is the latter who is the greater conqueror.

Sculpture in Lumbini: Surrounded by her attendants and gripping a tree,
the young Siddhartha's mother has just given birth to the future Buddha.

The Word

Better than a thousand senseless words

is a single sensible word

which can bring peace to him who hears it.

Siddhartha Gautama, who, as legend has it, began preaching at a very young age.

Through Ourselves

Through ourselves, in truth, evil is done.
Through ourselves we are sullied.
Through ourselves evil is avoided.
Through ourselves, in truth, we are purified.
Purity and impurity are personal, no one can purify another.

Frescoes adorning the caves of Ajanta: The young Buddha leads a life in which
women dancers and pleasures of the flesh play a large part.

To See

The world is blind.

Those who see are few.

The mind is difficult to master and unstable.

It goes where it will.

It is good to master it.

The mind mastered insures happiness.

Fresco in Ajanta: Is this the Buddha's wife, the beautiful Yasodhara?

On Imaginary Existence

If the disciple sees, sees things such as they are through right wisdom, he does not cherish ideas touching on the past: "Did I exist in the past? Did I not exist in the past? Who was I in the past?"

Nor does he cherish questions touching on the future: "Will I exist in the future? Will I not exist in the future? Who will I be in the future? How will I be in the future?"

Nor does he cherish doubts about himself touching on the present: "Am I? Am I not? How am I? As a living being, where do I come from? Where am I going?"

Such ideas do not arise in him.

One day he left and set off on one of time's paths.
Here, not far from Sarasvati (Saheth-Mahath).

Mental Acts

When there is an act that you would like to carry out with your mind, regarding this mental act you must think, "Will this act that I wish to carry out with my mind bring harm to me, or harm to others, or harm to both? Is this mental act awkward, does it lead to suffering, does it produce evil?"

If, in thinking this way, you conclude, "Yes, the mental act that I wish to carry out would bring harm to me, or harm to others, or harm to both, and in fact this awkward mental act would lead to suffering and produce evil," then such a mental act, O Rahula, ought not to be carried out."

Sculpture in the Lahore Museum: He did not find the truth while his ascetic practices left him closer to death than life.

On Thought

Just as a monkey frolicking in the forest seizes one branch, then immediately lets it go to grasp another, and still others in turn, so what you call thought, knowledge, O my disciples, forms and dissolves continuously.

Bodhgaya: Enlightenment came to him beneath the Bo, or Bodhi-tree, a magnificent Ficus religiosa that stands even today thanks to the care of pilgrims.

On War

All conquest creates hate because he who is conquered remains in hardship. He who holds to peace, having forsaken any idea of victory or defeat, stays happy.

Bodhgaya: The temple of the Enlightenment.

On the Fruit of Our Acts

A man may rob another as much as it serves his ends; yet robbed in turn by another, as robbed as he is, he robs the other still.

So long as the fruit of evil is not ripe the fool thinks, "Now is the time, now is my chance!" Yet when his act has borne fruit, everything goes awry for him. The killer is killed in turn; the conqueror encounters one who will conquer him; the insulter is insulted; the persecutor meets with difficulties.

Thus, through the evolution of the act, he who robs is robbed in turn.

He meditates here in the lotus position...

Humanity in Crisis

Nowadays, O Brahmin, people are inflamed with immoral desires, overcome with their depraved appetites, obsessed by false doctrines. This being so, they seize keen-edged swords and put each other to death, and many perish. Moreover, rain does not fall regularly on these inflamed, overcome, obsessed people. It is hard to have enough to eat. The crops are mediocre, moldy, stunted. And so many perish. Such is the reason, such is the cause of the seeming decline and growth of humanity. This is why villages are no longer villages, towns are no longer towns, cities are no longer cities, and the countryside is empty.

...and serenity fills his being. He is one with the universe.

Faults

The faults of others are easy to see; one's own are difficult to see. In truth, we carefully winnow the faults of others like chaff, whereas we cover our own, just as the wily gambler hides the trick that will prove his downfall.

Bodhgaya: The stylized footprint of the Buddha, who while walking meditated on whether he should teach or not.

On Controlling the Mind

The Buddha said to the monks:

"When the mind is controlled, it must be like the stone of the four orients: although this stone lies in the middle of the courtyard, the rain falls upon it but does not destroy it; the sun heats it but does not melt it; the wind blows yet cannot lift it. A mind under control resembles this stone."

Buddha preaching… and the fervor of women believers.

The Heart of Man

The heart of man is thus: one thought comes, another goes; like blades of grass and bits of wood, thoughts coming forward and those receding do not interfere with one another.

Above the sky and below there is no joy that is repeated.

Between the sky and the earth there is only a temporary abode.

Four Virtues

How are we to ford wild streams? How are we to cross oceans? How are we to be capable of abandoning suffering? And how can we obtain purity? The World Honored then recited these verses:

Bodhgaya: Has the countryside changed after twenty-five hundred years? Hardly.

It is with faith that one can ford streams.
It is with diligence that one crosses the ocean.
It is with energy that one can reject suffering.
And it is with wisdom that one obtains purity.

Wisdom

Monks, two things partake of wisdom, silence and interiority.

What does the development of silent calm within oneself produce? It allows consciousness to develop. And what good can be drawn from a developed consciousness? Desires are put in their proper perspective and can be forsaken.

And if interiority is developed, what good does that do? It allows wisdom to develop. And what good is developed wisdom? It leads one to forsake all manner of ignorance, to cut off ignorance at the root.

Consciousness troubled by desire cannot be freed; wisdom troubled by ignorance cannot be developed. Thus one can make one's desires disappear by freeing one's mind, and make ignorance disappear by freeing one's wisdom.

Sarnath: Here the Buddha taught his first four disciples.
Ruins of a monastery that he founded.

The World Honored said to them:

And in the same way, there are these five hindrances,
in the Discipline of the Noble One....

What are the five?

The hindrance of lustful desire,

The hindrance of malice,

The hindrance of sloth and idleness,

The hindrance of pride and self-righteousness,

The hindrance of doubt.

Ellora cave temples: The Buddha walking. Until the end of his days
he traveled over northern India teaching the practice of the right path.

The Infinite

The World Honored said to the monks:

There are four limitless thoughts. What are the four?

Love,

Compassion,

Sympathetic joy,

And equanimity.

Katmandu, Nepal: At every corner these statues are found.
*Here the Buddha is shown making a protective gesture (*mudra*).*

On Meditation

He who wishes to obtain the Way must sit in an empty and closed place. As he exhales and inhales he observes this movement of respiration: he knows if it is short or long. He observes with detachment the forms that appear, and he is fully conscious. Whether the breath is held or not, he observes, and he is conscious of all the forms that appear: he observes them one by one, and this is how he meditates. Whatever forms appear, he considers them from the outside, he considers them from the inside. While observing them and meditating, he feels joy.

If he happens to have a foreign thought, he must not linger over it. To have a heart free of desire and to follow the right Way is a rare pearl in this world; therefore, if in his heart there arises once again the least movement of desire, he must carefully stop it and immediately return to his practice. If he progresses with his mind in this way, he is like a man who owns a clouded mirror in which no image can be seen; by rubbing it he removes the grime and immediately images can be seen. He who has dismissed lustful desire, hate, and stupidity is like a mirror that has been rubbed clean. He now meditates attentively: "Under the sky there is nothing that is stable, nothing lasts forever."

Ajanta caves: The Buddha stricken with years.

On Death

O ld age and death come crushing one and all without the least distinction.

Grandees and priests, merchants and peasants, no one can escape or make light of it.

The danger is nigh: it buries each and everyone.

In that realm there is neither room nor use for war.

Victory cannot be had by deploying cavalry, or war chariots, or infantry, or sacred formulas, or wealth.

He who leads an upright life through his body, word, and thought will be respected here and now, all the world over; he will also find happiness of mind in the world to come.

Kushinagara: The end. The lion of enlightenment lies down in the so-called Pari-nirvana position.

The Lamp

Therefore, O Ananda, be lamps unto yourselves. Betake yourselves to no external refuge. Hold fast to the truth as a lamp. Hold fast as a refuge to the truth.... And whosoever, Ananda, either now or after I am dead, shall be a lamp unto themselves, and a refuge unto themselves, shall betake themselves to no external refuge, but holding fast to the truth as their lamp, and holding fast as their refuge to the truth, shall look not for refuge to any one besides themselves—it is they, Ananda, among my true disciples, who shall reach the very topmost Height!

Pari-nirvana as it is represented in a giant stone sculpture in Sri Lanka.

Vigilance

He who becomes watchful,

having been negligent,

illuminates the world like the moon

emerging from the clouds.

Jean-Louis Nou

The photographs facing the texts in this volume were taken on a voyage in October and November 1981 retracing the places that marked the Buddha's life. Here Jean-Louis Nou is seen standing in front of the giant stupa at Nalanda, the famous university founded by the Buddha's successors.

Jean-Louis Nou lost his life in an accident in 1992. This volume is dedicated to him.

Buddhism as a religion has almost completely disappeared from present-day India. Four great sites of pilgrimages remain, however: Lumbini, Siddhartha's birthplace; Bodhgaya, where he attained enlightenment; Sarnath, where he decided to begin teaching and set in motion the "wheel of Dhamma," or "Dharma," that is, the wheel of natural law (the site lies just a few miles from Benares, Varanisi in Hindi, India's greatest holy city); and finally Kasia (Kushinagara), where he died and was cremated. Many other shrines exist that either recall the Buddha's passage (he became a wandering monk), or attest to the splendor of Buddhist civilization (such as the painted caves of Ajanta near Bombay).

Selected Bibliography

Ch'en, Kenneth K. S. *Buddhism: The Light of Asia.* Hauppauge, N.Y.: Barron's Educational Series, 1968.

Conze, Edward. *Buddhist Scriptures.* London: Penguin, 1959.

Davids, T. W. Rhys, trans. *The Buddhist Suttas.* Delhi: Motilal Banarsidass, n.d.

De Bary, William Theodore. *The Buddhist Tradition.* New York: Vintage, 1972.

Embree, Ainslie. *The Hindu Tradition: Readings in Oriental Thought.* New York: Vintage, 1972.

Hanh, Thich Nhat. *Old Path White Clouds: Walking in the Footsteps of the Buddha.* Berkeley, Calif.: Parallax Press, 1991. (The life and teachings of Gautama Buddha drawn from twenty-four texts in Pali, Sanscrit, and Chinese.)

Mou-lam, Wong, and A. F. Price. *The Diamond Sutra and the Sutra of Hui-Neng.* Boston: Shambhala, 1990.

Smith, Huston. *The Illustrated World's Religions: A Guide to Our Wisdom Traditions.* San Francisco: HarperSan Francisco, 1991.